The Inner Circle

Studying The Lives
Of 13 Apostles

E. Dale Click

CSS Publishing Company, Inc., Lima, Ohio

THE INNER CIRCLE

Copyright © 2000 by
CSS Publishing Company, Inc.
Lima, Ohio

Library of Congress Cataloging-in-Publication Data

Click, E. Dale.
  The inner circle : studying the lives of 13 apostles / E. Dale Click.
       p.   cm.
  Includes bibliographical references.
  ISBN 0-7880-1590-7 (pbk. : alk. paper)
  1. Apostles—Biography.   I. Title.
BS2440.C53 2000
225.9'22—dc21
[B]   99-055448

ISBN 0-7880-1590-7
PRINTED IN U.S.A.

*In grateful appreciation
to sons, Barry and Dean,
both disciples of Christ,
and from whom I have learned much about life,
in this era of truncated faith.*

Table Of Contents

Preface

Inviting people to submit subjects for a series of studies revealed strong interest in the lives of the apostles and Paul. Paul, of course, was not one of the original twelve apostles. He is rightly called an apostle, however, since he was the first great missionary of the Church. Some of the questions asked were: Who are the apostles? Why did Jesus select these twelve men? What did they accomplish after the resurrection? What happened to them? What can we learn from them? I became as curious as the questioners. Considerable research resulted, including a journey to the Holy Land to give me fresh insights.

The list of the twelve apostles differs in the synoptic Gospels (Matthew, Mark, Luke) and in the Book of Acts. For their names, read Mark 3:16-19; Matthew 10:2-4; Luke 6:14-16; and Acts 1:13. Acts necessarily lists eleven, as Luke describes the development of the Early Church after Judas' death. The Gospel of John does not include a list of the twelve.

The differences in the lists are not in the people referred to but in the names. In New Testament times people used more than one name. We can solve the differences by concluding that Matthew and Levi are the same person; that Thaddaeus and Judas, the son of James, are one and the same person; and that Bartholomew and Nathaniel are one and the same person. When we discuss these disciples, however, we shall be more specific on the background of names.

Knowledge of the lives of the apostles can enrich lives in this present day. They teach us lessons about life. They are lived examples of the workings of the Holy Spirit. All (except Judas) inspire and motivate us to a higher level of commitment; and all, including Judas, give us a glimpse of God's hope for our lives. Ordinary people of extraordinary faith, the apostles laid the foundations for what the Church rightly calls the Apostolic Faith.

Chapter 1

The Life Of Peter

We readily identify Peter; his name heads the list of disciples in each of the biblical references.

A boat ride on the Sea of Galilee is exhilarating. While most passengers sat in the cabin of the small ship, I went on deck to feel the gentle breeze on my face. Excitement tingled down my spine. On this body of water on which our Lord sailed with his disciples, my eye cast about drinking in the beautiful scenery of lake and mountains. At the far end of the lake is Capernaum — Peter's hometown. As we docked, I imagined Peter coming home with a boatload of fish. I visualized Jesus and the disciples docking at Capernaum.

Peter's house in Capernaum was just a stone's throw from the synagogue. It gave me the impression that here was a family man, dedicated to God, caring for a flourishing fishing business, with several partners and a fleet of boats. Our Lord called Peter, a person who surrendered his own invested interests, to follow him. After the resurrection, when Peter became an itinerant preacher, tradition has him traveling to several lands. His wife accompanied him and died with him on a cross in the city of Rome. It all began at Capernaum when Jesus called Peter to become a fisher of people.

Peter was a Galilean. Josephus, Jewish scholar and historian (37? - 95?), is a reliable source for background. For a time, Josephus was Governor of Galilee. He knew what the Galileans were like. He wrote: "They were very fond of innovations, and by nature disposed to changes, and delighted in seditions.... They were ever ready to follow a leader and to begin an insurrection."[1] Josephus also pointed out that the Galileans had quick tempers and quarreled often, yet most were chivalrous. "The Galileans have never been destitute of courage," he concluded.

William Barclay cites the Talmud's description of Galileans: "They were ever more anxious for honor than for gain." Barclay adds: "Quick-tempered, impulsive, emotional, easily aroused by an appeal to adventure, loyal to the end — Peter was a typical man of Galilee."[2]

Is this not the Peter we meet in the scriptures? It prompts us to reevaulate the credentials of a Christian: one does not have to be perfect to become a follower of Jesus Christ. Quick tempers, quarrelsome tongues, and emotional actions are not necessary traits for Christians. But God does call people to project his will among people. Followers of Christ are not prefabricated in heaven. Followers of Christ come from dust and return to dust.

Much of Peter's life prior to the crucifixion is discernible in the Gospels. Those who knew him called him Simon. Jesus gave him the name Peter (Cephas). Andrew had brought his brother to meet Jesus. Jesus said, "You are Simon the son of John? You are to be called Cephas" (which is translated Peter).[3] Peter is the Greek and Cephas is the Aramaic and both mean "Rock."

Mark's Gospel gives other clues. Papias, Bishop of Hierapolis (second century), records how Mark's Gospel was written: "Mark, having become the interpreter of Peter, wrote down accurately everything that he remembered, without however recording in order what was said or done by Christ. For neither did he hear the Lord speak, nor did he follow him, but afterwards ... he followed Peter, who adapted his instruction to the needs of his hearers, but had no design of givng a connected account of the Lord's oracles. So then Mark made no mistake while he thus wrote some things down as he remembered them, for he made it his one care not to omit anything that he had heard, or to set down any false statement therein."[4]

It was Peter who uttered memorable words when Jesus asked his disciples if they also would desert him: "Lord, to whom can we go? You have the words of eternal life. We have come to believe and know that you are the Holy One of God" (John 6:67-69).

It was of Peter our Lord said, "You are Peter, and on this rock I will build my church, and the gates of Hades will not prevail against it" (Matthew 16:18). Upon the lives of such believers the Church stands.

It was Peter who was rebuked sternly by our Lord when Peter tried to dissuade him from going to Jerusalem. Said Jesus, "Get behind me, Satan! You are a stumbling block to me; for you are setting your mind not on divine things but on human things" (Matthew 16:23). At that moment, Jesus may have visualized his wilderness experience when Satan tried to derail him. He would not let Peter derail him either. Determination and purpose are some of the secrets of the inner stuff of Jesus' life.

The incident we remember most and hide behind often is Peter's denial in the courtyard prior to the crucifixion. Not once but three times, Peter vowed he never knew Jesus. And we take courage because our Lord forgave him. How do we know this? Because after the resurrection Jesus pointedly sought out Peter. Jesus' third appearance to the disciples at a seaside breakfast (John 21) reflects Jesus' concern for Peter.

It was Peter who first entered the tomb. It was Peter who suggested another apostle be chosen to replace Judas. It was Peter who preached the first Christian sermon and thus became the spokesperson for the young Church. It was Peter, along with John, who healed the lame man at the beautiful gate of the temple (Acts 3:1-11). It was Peter who traveled to Samaria and preached the gospel. It was Peter who dealt with the false ministry of Simon Magus (Acts 8:14-24), and who dealt with the duplicity of Anania and Sapphira (Acts 5:1-11).

There is no doubt of the strong and courageous leadership of Peter. Beyond the pages of the New Testament come stories connecting him with Antioch and stating that he became that church's bishop for seven years. They say Peter preached in Asia Minor also.

Most researchers agree that Peter went to Rome about A.D. 61, almost thirty years after the resurrection, and was crucified there. His preaching likely caused the concubines of Agrippa, the Prefect, and the wife of Albinas, the favorite of the Emperor, to turn away from their sordid roles in life. If so, Peter was one of the first to liberate women. In any event, it made Agrippa and Albinas

11

furious, and they determined to kill Peter. Peter was warned by friends to seek safety. But as Peter was fleeing Rome, he had a vision of Jesus entering Rome. "Lord," he said, "whither goest thou? (*Domine, quo vadis?*) The Lord answered, "I go into Rome to be crucified...." "Lord," said Peter, "art thou being crucified again?" "Yea, Peter," said the Lord, "I am being crucified again."[5]

So Peter understood that Jesus was going into Rome to bear the cross from which he was running. Peter went back to Rome to die. They crucified his wife first, thereby inflicting further pain upon Peter. Peter encouraged her, "Remember the Lord."[6] With courage Peter faced his own death. His jailer became a Christian as a result of his witness. Peter requested that he be crucified downwards. He felt unworthy to die as his Lord had died.

Whatever we relate about Peter, we must say he gave every area of his life to Christ. He held nothing back. Reckless at times? Yes. Make mistakes? Yes. Exercise poor judgment? Yes. Risk taker? Yes. Overall, Peter was a person of raw spiritual courage, a believer undaunted when the going got tough, a person who practiced what he believed.

These lessons we can learn from the life of Peter:

1) Whatever success you attain in your chosen vocation, there is more to life than making a living. Fishing isn't the Alpha and Omega.

2) Use your knowledge and skill as a supplement to your real calling — to live today for what is worthwhile.

3) Although you may believe Christ will come again, as Peter believed in the coming of the Messiah, be alert to the presence of the living Christ now. He is breathing down your neck. Recognize Jesus on the road and on the run! When forgiveness is necessary, God will be the first by your side.

5) Be a person of purpose, believing all things work for the good of those who love the Lord. Read Romans 8:28.

6) If you find yourself denying your Lord, remember he never denies you. Wake up when the cock crows! Rush to an empty tomb. Get going for the Lord. Satan always wants us to languish in our failures. God wants us to taste abundant living. That's the difference between belief and unbelief.

7) When it is time to die, die with dignity. Be a witness to the reality of the resurrection. There is more to life than death. We have eternity ahead of us.

Questions For Discussion

1. Define "apostle."

2. Does being one of the twelve automatically make a person an apostle?

3. What is the difference between a disciple and an apostle?

4. "Discipline" derives from "disciple." Are we disciples? Are we disciplined?

5. Why were not women named apostles?

6. What were some of the skills of Peter?

7. What is the force of forgiveness?

8. What was the sin of Simon Magus? Of Anania and Sapphira? Are there such sins in the church today?

9. After leaving the industry of fishing, did Peter have an income?

10. What inspiration do you experience from the life of Peter?

---

1. Josephus, Life, 17; *Wars of the Jews*, 3,3,2.

2. William Barclay, *The Master's Men* (Abingdon Press), p. 18.

3. John 1:42, from the word for rock in Aramaic (*kepha*) and Greek (*petra*), respectively.

4. *The New Schaff-Herzog Encyclopedia Of Religious Knowledge*, Vol. VIII, (Baker 1950), p. 337.

5. Acts of Peter, p. 35.

6. See Eusebius, Ecclesiastical History.

Chapter Two

The Life Of Andrew

Andrew is rightfully remembered as the introducer. Many of us find it easier to introduce a stranger to Jesus than to introduce a member of our household. Andrew began with his family. "He (Andrew) first found his brother Simon and said to him, 'We have found the Messiah' (which is translated Anointed or Christ)" (John 1:41).

As we study the lives of a group of people who changed the world during the first century, keep in focus the fact that there was a wide range of personalities among the disciples. God uses all types of people to herald Good News.

The word *apostle* in Greek means "one who has been sent." Jesus called people to his side who were not only good listeners but proactive. In Mark 3:14 is the record: "And he (Jesus) appointed twelve, whom he also named apostles, to be with him, and to be sent out to proclaim the message...." Of all the twelve, Andrew typifies more than any other the words *sent out*. According to the Gospel of John, Andrew was the first of the twelve to follow Jesus (John 1:35-40). The Early Church often referred to Andrew as *Protokletos* (the *First-called*).

In biblical times families were listed according to fathers' names. Matthew began his book by describing Jesus' geneology as "... the son of David, the son of Abraham" and lists 42 generations. Would that we could list our ancestors so readily, as Alex Haley wished had been done for him. Haley found it necessary to journey to Africa to trace his family history. Some can date their family history to the *Mayflower* or even further. I succumbed to buying a book people peddle about one's ancestors. I intended to place a family tree plaque over the mantel but quickly discarded the idea when I learned the name *Click* means "one who talks incessantly."

Andrew's father was Jonah. Andrew is usually referred to as Peter's brother. Foremost, Andrew was the son of Jonah. *Jonah* also means John, as in John 1:42. *Jonah* means "dove." *John* means "Jehovah hath been gracious." Nothing more is known about the father of Andrew and Peter.

Jonah or John lived in Bethsaida. *Bethsaida* means "house of fishers." It was aptly named since it was situated on the north shore of the Sea of Galilee. Three disciples came from this town: Philip, Andrew, and Peter. Bethsaida was near the site of the feeding of the five thousand (Mark 6:45 and Luke 9:10), and where Jesus healed a blind man (Mark 8:22). Bethsaida was the capital city of Herod Philip (4 B.C. to A.D. 34). Jesus' ministry failed there, however. That's why he cried, "Woe to you, Chorazin! Woe to you, Bethsaida! For if the deeds of power done in you had been done in Tyre and Sidon, they would have repented long ago, sitting in sackcloth and ashes. But at the judgment it will be more tolerable for Tyre and Sidon than for you" (Luke 10:13, 14). Jesus was referring to the pagan section of the capital city and not to the older Jewish section. It was a city inhabited by Jews and Gentiles. It maintained close business and cultural ties with Galilee where Herod Philip's brother, Antipas, ruled. It is quite possible that Andrew and Peter spoke Greek as well as Aramaic. They grew up in a culture shaped by both Jewish and Gentile life.

Andrew was a fisherman by trade. He and his brother Peter, and their friends James and John were in partnership. By now both Andrew and Peter resided in Capernaum, a few miles from Bethsaida, still on the shore of the Sea of Galilee.

Andrew, a conscientious Jew, had not been turned on by the legalism of his religion. John the Baptist turned him on. Andrew was baptized by John the Baptist and became a follower of the Baptist. Andrew was open, pliable, and teachable. When truth dawned upon him, he had to share it. That's why Andrew is called the first evangelist. When John the Baptist pointed to Jesus as the Messiah, Andrew followed Jesus, inquired more from him, and then introduced his brother to Jesus.

Books on birth order give some possible clue to the personalities of Peter and Andrew. The firstborn, as Peter, are often leaders. The secondborn, as Andrew, are frequently followers. Andrew never appears to be jealous of Peter's foremost role among the disciples. He seems content to take second place. He doesn't give the first sermon of the newly-born church; his brother, Peter, does. But assuredly Andrew fulfilled the commission to be "sent out."

What we know about the acts of Andrew from the Bible are simple acts. He introduces people to Jesus. First, he brought a member of his own household. That's not easy to do. How many wives or husbands have prayed for the conversion of their spouse? There is a yearning to give the best to those closest to us. Christmas observances often bring the best and the worst out of us. For example, we often see well-intentioned parents flooding their children with electronic gadgets. What we give our children on such occasions does not count as much as what we give them daily in terms of faith and hope and love. I remember my father not so much for the green bicycle he bought me but for the fact that when he got out of bed on a Sunday morning there was no question where he was going — he was going to church.

We think of Peter as bold, and so he was. But Andrew was bold, too. He didn't hesitate to invite his brother to a new life with the Messiah. He was bold in faith also. He unashamedly believed in Jesus as the one who saves, who translates truth into everyday terms. Andrew embraced Jesus' illustration, "For the gate is narrow and the road is hard that leads to life, and there are few who find it" (Matthew 7:14). Andrew found it and wanted everybody to walk through that gate — a personal relationship with a living Savior.

Secondly, Andrew answered questions directly. In order to do this, you must know something of significance. Andrew appears to have devoured the faith Jesus offered. Philip, however, could not translate truth so easily. A couple Greeks approached Philip and asked him about Jesus. Philip did not seem to know exactly what to do or say so he asked Andrew for help. Andrew didn't hesitate. He took the Greeks to Jesus. He knew Jesus would talk to anybody who would listen. And Jesus told the Greeks, "Whoever serves me, the Father will honor" (John 12:26).

Thirdly, Andrew never hesitated to offer anyone or anything to Jesus. When the thousands of people followed Jesus into the hills without thinking about food or the clock because they were intensely interested in what he had to say, it was Jesus who became concerned about mealtime: "Where are we to buy bread for these people to eat?" (John 6:5). It was Andrew who supplied the answer although at the time he had no idea what would occur. Andrew burst out almost facetiously, "There is a boy here who has five barley loaves and two fish. But what are they among so many people?" (John 6:9). But he didn't hesitate to offer what was available. That attitude often results in miracles. In this instance, thousands were fed by the hand of Jesus.

No wonder Andrew is loved! He is a person we all might endeavor to imitate — introducing people to Jesus, answering questions which result in action, and offering what is available.

Barclay's preface in *The Master's Men*, makes this observation about traditions: "I am far from claiming that ... traditions and legends have any claims to being history; but they have their importances, for the stories which circulate about a man (person) tell us a great deal about that man (person), even when they are not factually true."

Three nations love Andrew. There is the tradition recorded by Eusebius (Eusebius of Caesarea or Eusebius Pamphili, c. 266-340?, Greek historian, called the Father of Ecclesiastical History) that Andrew went to Scythia, southern Russia in the Black Sea area, where he was stoned and crucified. He became the patron saint of Russia until the communist regime destroyed all of that. Nevertheless, there are people in Russia today whose faith is very much alive because of the memory of Andrew.

Another country which reveres Andrew is Greece. Most scholars agree that Andrew was crucified there. The cross shaped like an X symbolizes Andrew, for he reportedly died on a cross of that shape.

The third country is Scotland. In the fifth century Saint Regulus is supposed to have taken relics of Andrew's body and buried them in a place that was later called Saint Andrew's. I was reminded of this as I played the course at Saint Andrew's, the birthplace of golf. I was told the Scots chuckle about Andrew as being their patron saint because he "borrowed" a boy's lunch — a free lunch and gave it to the master. Jesus got the lunch "Scot" free!

David A. MacLennan tells us that "... the flag used by General George Washington at Cambridge, Massachusetts, on January 9, 1776, was composed of thirteen alternate red and white stripes with the combined crosses of Saint Andrew and Saint George in a field of blue in place of stars. Also, in the 29th degree, the ancient accepted Scottish Rite of Freemasonry is known as the order of 'Grand Scottish Knight of St. Andrew.' "[1]

These lessons we can learn from Andrew:

1) Be willing to have others increase and yourself decrease. A secondary role often gets the job done.

2) Beware of what resentment and jealousy can do to the human mind and heart. Humility is a healthier way.

3) Introduce people to Jesus, whether relative or stranger. Be bold for Jesus. One of the best ways is to invite and bring people to worship. Ask people what church they belong to. If they are members of a church different from yours, rejoice and exchange ideas. If they are not members of a church, invite them to your church. Be specific. Set a date and time to go to worship together.

4) Offer what you have to the Lord. From a little can come much. The Empire State Building, begun in the midst of a depression, began with one stone, and still stands today despite an airplane that crashed into it.

5) Go anywhere anytime for the Lord. We are "sent out" also. It may lead to a cross. More likely it will lead to abundant living and death with dignity.

Questons For Discussion

1. Was Andrew a leader or a follower? What are the characteristics of a leader? A follower?

2. If evangelism is a trait of Andrew, why aren't there more Andrews? What are the characteristics of an evangelist?

3. Do you suppose the parents of Peter and Andrew thought more of one than the other? What are the consequences of showing favoritism?

4. Does the Church reverence both Peter and Andrew? Leader or follower, what are the marks of being a servant of the Lord?

5. What makes Andrew lovable?

6. What do you do about failure? Jesus failed at Bethsaida. Why? What did he do about it?

---

1. David A. MacLennan, *Twelve Who Changed The World*, p. 37.

Chapter 3

The Lives Of James And John

Apostles James and John are always linked together. They were brothers. Their father's name was Zebedee, a name which means "Jehovah has given." Zebedee was a man of some prominence in the community, a successful businessman in the important industry of fishing. The mother of James and John was Salome. There is reason to believe that Salome was the sister of Mary, the mother of Our Lord. If so, James and John were cousins of Jesus. Salome witnessed the crucifixion of Jesus as reported in Matthew 27:56. We do not hear anymore about Zebedee.

Thus, James and John came from a rather well-to-do family with a home located somewhere near the Sea of Galilee. They had servants. The young men were obedient sons. They learned the business of their father, which must have pleased Zebedee. Fathers have a penchant for that kind of thing, sons following in their footsteps.

James was the older of the two. The birth order books are not 100 percent accurate when it comes to James and John. James seems to take a back seat to John, similar to the way Andrew did with his brother, Peter. Here are two sets of brothers on the team of Jesus. Brothers do not always get along. Jealousy often reigns. Envy can play havoc with the family. To the credit of these sets of brothers, there do not appear to be such problems. They are loyal not only to Christ but to each other. That must have been beautiful to behold. There is nothing like genuine brotherly love.

There is not much known about James. Yet, he is usually listed among the first three of the apostles — Peter, James, and John — in that order. These three appear to be the inner core of the apostolic band.

James and John were typical Galileans. Scripture reveals them to be impulsive and quick-tempered. Jesus called them *Boanerges*, Sons of Thunder (Mark 3:17). Jesus did not select perfect people to be his followers. He chose people, however, of some depth of character, people capable of growth and open to expanded ideas.

James was the first of the twelve to become a martyr. In Acts 12:2 "... King Herod laid violent hands upon some who belonged to the church. He had James, the brother of John, killed with the sword."

Eusebius, the historian, records a story about James and his influence upon others, even those who spoke against him. He says that "... the one who led James to the judgment seat, when he saw him bearing his testimony, was moved and confessed that he also was a Christian. They were both, therefore, Clement says, led away together; and on the way he begged James to forgive him. And he, after considering a little said: 'Peace be with thee,' and kissed him. And thus they were both beheaded at the same time."[1]

It was because of such witnesses as James, the Christian faith spread to all corners of the earth.

James is the partron saint of Spain. There is no foundation to this story but it reflects something of the character of James. He is supposed to have gone to Spain and preached the resurrected Christ. He returned to Palestine but after his execution by Herod, James' body was taken back to Spain and strange things happened, including a vision of the Virgin Mary coming to James to encourage and strengthen him. Even to this day in Saragossa, Spain, a hundred lamps are kept burning to remember this occurrence.

What is more important is to remember James as a person whose character contained some ingredients helpful to us:

1) James had that wonderful combination of courage and forgiveness.

2) As with Andrew, he didn't have a jealous streak in his body.

3) James was a person of great faith, able to witness to the risen Lord even at the time of his violent death.

22

John's story is different. It is a story of change. *The Christian Century* had a succession of articles on "How My Mind Has Changed" by noted Christian scholars on various subjects. These articles revealed quite a switch among some. Yet, our human nature never seems to change. As a pastor, I wonder at times what good we ever do. There seems to be so little change in people as far as their character is concerned despite our preaching and teaching. I could list set types of people that have been in each of the five parishes I have served. Council meetings, for example, are almost predictable. There are always the same few people who are going to be against a new proposal. And, I look at myself and wonder how much I have changed over the years. I suppose I have mellowed a bit, although some would be hard pressed to notice it! I suppose I don't take some things as threateningly as I used to do. But, have I really changed?

Change is another word for growth. People who do not want to see change, either in a parish or within the heart, are almost always people who have become stagnant in their thinking and outlook.

Not so with John. Take a look at his growth. Discipleship cost John his violent temper. Yes, I know he is more often remembered as the "beloved disciple" and the disciple Jesus loved (John 13:23). But it wasn't always that way with John.

After all, John was a businessman — a fisherman. Professional fishermen can be a tough lot. At the mouth of the Amazon in Brazil (stranded there for three days because my airplane from Rio de Janeiro to Caraccas lost an engine), I saw fishing boats come in, laden with their homemade nets. There was a quarrel. One man lost his front teeth. Another man lost his fish. I didn't see anything that resembled the commandment of love!

John may not have been as violent. But Jesus would not have called these brothers "Sons of Thunder" had he not seen their hair-trigger tempers. For example, because a village in Samaria would not welcome Jesus, John and his brother, James, said, "Lord, do you want us to command fire to come down from heaven and consume them?" (Luke 9:54). For that outburst of temper they were rebuked by Jesus. Discipleship cost John his violent temper. There is a price tag on Christian love.

Discipleship cost John his intolerant heart. Because John saw a man casting out demons in Christ's name, John took him to task and forbad him to do so. John did not think this fellow belonged in the same league or as he said, "... he does not follow with us" (Luke 9:49). Jesus' reply was direct: "Do not stop him; for whoever is not against you is for you" (Luke 9:50). John had to give up intolerance. There is a price tag on Christian love.

Discipleship cost John uncontrolled ambition. The disciples had an argument. James and John wanted to be center pieces in Jesus' kingdom, by sitting at the right and the left of Jesus "... in your glory" (see Mark 10:35-45). Jesus settled the matter. "But it is not so among you; but whoever wishes to become great among you must be your servant, and whoever wishes to be first among you must be slave of all" (Mark 10:43-44). John had to have his ambition redirected. There is a price tag on Christian love.

Christian love changed John. John experienced what it meant to be loved by God. He became first a disciple and second a fisherman.

The transformation took place by association with our Lord in the climate of Christianity in action. Love divine excelled. The parable of the talents taught him that loving God meant giving a good account of time, ability, and possessions. The cleansing of the Temple taught him that God's house is for prayer and not a place to transact business. The feeding of the thousands taught him that God supplied. The parable of the good shepherd taught him the meaning of God's watchful care.

So John's character was molded into the shape of Christian love. He evidently leaned on the chest of Jesus at the Last Supper (John 13:24). He was given the honor of caring for Jesus' mother (John 19:26-27). He was the first of the disciples to arrive at the tomb (John 20:4).

John's Chistian love permeated the New Testament Church. In company with Peter, a lame man was healed. Along with Peter, he was imprisoned. Paul spoke of John as one of the great leaders of the Church (Galatians 2:9). It is his Gospel that warms the heart and comes with the strength of an eagle. Tradition has John ministering in Ephesus where he provided a home for Jesus' mother,

Mary. Persecuted by Rome, banished to the Isle of Patmos, John left a trail of mixing life with Christian love, mixing business and religion, mixing change and growth.

The lives of these disciples, James and John, tell us that our faith has a price tag. James gave his life. John lived until his nineties, the only apostle to do so, grew older gracefully, and likely wrote the Book of Revelation.

A lay person visited a great city church in Ohio during a business trip. After the worship, he congratulated the minister on the worship and his sermon. "But," said the manufacturer, "if you were my salesman, I'd discharge you. You got my attention by your appearance, voice, and manner; your prayer, reading and logical discourse aroused my interest; you warmed my heart with a desire for what you preached; and then — you stopped without asking me to do something about it! In business, the important thing is to get them to sign on the dotted line."[2]

Here is the dotted line I invite you to sign, as we have thought about the lives of James and John:

1) Can you love the person who got the position you knew you deserved?

2) Can you love the person who says you will be replaced?

3) Can you love the most obnoxious person you know?

4) Can you love that special person you are sure is out to get you?

5) Can you have forgiveness as well as courage, and courage as well as forgiveness?

6) Can you believe despite the lack of evidence?

7) Will you change and grow?

There is the bottom line. There is a price tag on Christian love. As Christians we are expected to change and grow. To love at the most inconvenient of times and to love the most unlovely people is our business. "By this everyone will know that you are my disciples, if you have love for one another" (John 13:35).

Questions For Discussion

1. What is the bottom line of your Christian faith?

2. What is Christian love? Describe and differentiate between the different kinds of love.

3. Was it right of Jesus to have an inner circle of disciples? How do you suppose the other disciples felt about that?

4. Do you want to be like James or John? Who is your Christian hero or heroine?

5. Why are some people "touch people" and others standoffish?

6   Do you think "hugging" in church is a good practice? What if you are not a hugger?

---

1. Reported by William Barclay, *The Master's Men* (Abingdon Press), p. 101.

2. Cited in *The Brethren Missionary Herald.*

Chapter 4

The Lives Of Philip
And Nathaniel/Bartholomew

Living in southern California in the days when there were no "self-service" gasoline stations, I used to purchase gas at a certain service station, going out of my way at times in order to do so. The attendant impressed me. He was and still is an actor. I saw him then and still do on television, mostly in commercials. He had a part interest in that service station. When he waited on you, it seemed you were the only person he was interested in for the rest of the day. Not only would he wipe the windshield but he would clean the windows inside and out, unless you stopped him because of being in a hurry. He always had a smile. He made me feel good. Owen, the service station attendant, was a likable fellow. He had the human touch. (Too bad we have lost that personal touch. Now at some stations we have to pay before we pump gas since they do not trust motorists anymore, and with good cause — a sign of our warped age.)

When Jesus was selecting people to follow him, the first one he called was Philip. Philip must have had some of the qualities of that service station attendant, Owen. There is some evidence of this in the scriptures. Philip had a friend, Nathaniel or Bartholomew, as we will point out later. Philip told him he had found the Messiah. He didn't argue when Nathaniel/Bartholomew was not immediately convinced. He simply said, "Come and see" (John 1:46). People who reflect the thrill of discovery and tell others about it have the quality of enthusiasm. Like Andrew, Philip was somewhat of a glad-hander, in the best sense.

This Philip, the apostle, is not the same as the one referred to in Acts 6:5, one of the seven. This apostle came from Bethsaida, the home of Andrew and Peter as well. In all likelihood he was a fisherman too, since this was the chief occupation in that region on the north shore of the Sea of Galilee. The books of Matthew, Mark, and Luke record his name. John, of course, does not list the apostles. John does record the calling of Philip in 1:43 when Jesus was in Galilee and "He found Philip and said to him, 'Follow me.' "

Philip was the one Jesus consulted on the occasion of feeding the five thousand. It is possible Philip was in charge of arranging the food and lodging for the twelve and Jesus, and that could be why Jesus turned to Philip with the question about how all these people were to be fed. In those days a denarii was equal to a day's pay. When Philip, with his calculator mind, answered, "Six months' wages would not buy enough bread for each of them to get a little," he knew what he was talking about. He saw the situation as impossible. Philip was warm-hearted and was the kind of person who would give you the shirt off his back, but he was also pessimistic. He wanted to do for people but he could not see how it could be done. Camillo Benso di Cavour (1810-61), great Italian statesman, stated that the supreme essential of a statesman is "a sense of the possible." It took not only the feeding of the five thousand but the resurrection to give Philip that extra dimension — a sense of the possible.

Another trait in Philip that needed developing is illustrated at the time the Greeks sought out Philip and wanted to be introduced to Jesus. Philip sought the aid of Andrew. It reveals something in Philip that makes us wonder if he disliked responsibility or that he pulled back from making important decisions. It could be he was the kind of person who let things slide or was just better at referrals. In any event, Philip knew his own weakness and dealt with it. One of the worst things a person can do is trick oneself.

In John 14:8 Philip speaks up and asks Jesus, "Lord, show us the Father, and we shall be satisfied." Jesus replied, "Have I been with you all this time, Philip, and you still do not know me? Whoever has seen me has seen the Father. How can you say, 'Show us the Father'?"

Philip must have used that experience as an illustration in his preaching and teaching, following the resurrection and Pentecost. Legends take him to Lydia, Asia, Parthia, and Gaul. Most agree he was a great leader of Asia and that he was martyred at Hierapolis, a city of Asia Minor located in the upper Lycus valley close to the hot springs of Pamukkale. His death is connected with a time when he found people worshiping a snake and endeavored to teach them differently. They say he was stripped, pierced in the ankles and thighs, and hung head downwards to die. He was faithful unto death. Imperfect traits of character did not deter faithful witness.

When we refer to Nathaniel or Bartholomew, we have difficulty concerning the name. Bartholomew was usually a second name, a name that identified him as a son (*Bar* means son) of Tolmai or Talmai. Nathaniel could have been his first name. Matthew, Mark, and Luke do not mention Nathaniel and John never mentions Bartholomew — thus, the confusion. In the Synoptics and Acts, Philip and Bartholomew occur together. As previously noted, Philip brought Nathaniel to Jesus. Since these two names appear in similar circumstance, it is reasonable to assume that Bartholomew and Nathaniel are the same person.

Jerome (c. 340-420), one of the Latin Fathers of the Church and a great Christian scholar, believed Bartholomew came from a long line of royalty. Maybe so. It is also said that after the resurrection Bartholomew preached in India, although this is highly doubtful. He could have preached in Phyrgia and Armenia.

In any event, he came from Cana in Galilee where Jesus changed water into wine at the marriage feast (John 2:1-11). When Philip told him that Jesus came from Nazareth, Nathaniel/Barthomew had difficulty believing it. Cana and Nazareth were neighboring villages. How could anyone coming from one of those insignificant villages, and especially from Nazareth, be the Messiah? Possibly there was a little hometown jealousy and contempt in Nathaniel/Bartholomew's comment.

When Jesus said he saw Nathaniel/Bartholomew under a fig tree, that had some meaning. A fig tree is about fifteen feet high and about 25 feet wide. It was a custom to have a fig tree outside one's door. It was like adding a family room to the house. The houses were small, like cottages. A fig tree was a place where one could go to rest, like sitting out on the front porch swing in the early evening. It was the kind of place to go when one wanted to be alone. It was a place for prayer and thoughtful thinking. In some sense, Jesus was saying he saw Nathaniel in prayer.

Thus, we can assume Nathaniel was a person well acquainted with scripture and a seeker of truth. He was also a sincere person. He did not immediately believe but he was willing to be convinced. He was a person with an open ear. There are those who are willing to see only what they want to see, and, there are those who are teachable. Nathaniel/Bartholomew was teachable.

Furthermore, Nathaniel/Bartholomew was a person who, when convinced, gave it his all. There was nothing half measure about him. After Jesus replied to his question, "Where did you get to know me?" by saying, "I saw you under the fig tree before Philip called you," he replied enthusiastically, "Rabbi, you are the Son of God. You are the King of Israel!" (John 1:48, 49).

It is likely Nathaniel/Bartholomew told that story about himself many times. A person of prayer, who surrendered his life to Christ, was also a person of staying power. He was with the other apostles after the resurrection (John 21:2). In some sense, he was a complete person. He died a martyr's death, possibly in India. He was one of the most adventurous of our apostles.

We can learn these things from the lives of Philip and Nathaniel/Bartholomew:

1)   Serve the Lord despite deficiencies in character — the Lord calls each of us!

2)   Think of others before you think of yourself.

3)   Introduce your friends to the living Christ and learn to do it as easily as you introduce a new friend to a long acquaintance.

4)   Ask questions but also listen to reasonable answers; in other words, be open-minded.

5)   Turn pessimism into possibilities.

6)   Assume rightful responsibilities even if a task is toilsome.

7) Refer matters when it is beyond your knowledge or experience.

8) Speak up when you do not know the answer even if a question may seem ludicrous to others.

9) Pray under some fig tree.

10) Search the scriptures.

11) Speak with the ring of sincerity.

12) Stick to your faith despite the foreboding times.

13) Be a complete person.

Years ago when I traveled in other countries teaching pastors and lay people evangelism, often I would conclude a message with words that appeared in the *United Church of Canada Magazine* and were found in the pocket of the late principal John M. Millar of the Theological Seminary, St. Stephen's College, University of Alberta, Edmonton. They were important words to me then and seem appropriate in reference to the lives of the apostles:

> *I heard him call,*
> *"Come follow," that was all;*
> *my gold grew dim,*
> *my soul went after him*
> *I rose and followed, that was all;*
> *who would not follow*
> *if he heard his call?*

———————————

Questions For Discussion

1. What is meant by "a call"?

2. Are only apostles and present-day ordained ministers called? What should "a call" mean to a lay person?

3. What does it mean to become a person of prayer?

4. What are the marks of an apostle?

5. If there are blemishes in our character, and admittedly there are, how do we deal with them?

6. What is meant by "a complete person"?

Chapter 5

The Lives Of Thomas And Matthew

The best creed ever confessed came from the lips of Thomas, "My Lord and my God!" (John 20:28). Yet Thomas is not remembered for a creed; we use his name to describe a person's attitude. We call anyone who does not accept readily what others accept quickly a Doubting Thomas.

We ought to thank God for the doubting Thomases of history. Hippocrites, called the Father of Medicine, doubted disease stemmed from the heathen gods and that disease could be cured by magic. Because of his doubts, disease came to be understood as a natural event which follows natural laws.

Not one of us could survive on surmises. We must investigate; we must be sure, proceeding only after all the data is at hand. Who could imagine a business guessing about its gross receipts for the past month! We must put our hands on the facts. We must be able to place our finger on a problem. Coleridge (1772-1834, English poet) once stated, "Until you question, you do not believe; you believe that you believe."

When it comes to religion, we tend to become impatient with the questioner or a person who does not readily accept our explanation of God. We give up on people rather easily: "What's the use — he'll never believe." What is actually the case is that we have difficulty articulating the faith so that others can readily understand and appreciate what we believe. Or it could be that "we do not believe; we believe that we believe."

A promising, bright young man of my church went off to college for the first time. Raised in the Sunday school, catechized, the possessor of church attendance awards, and instructed to accept God, he stepped into his first college class. The professor startled him by saying that the Bible is a book of fables. In a matter of

33

weeks the young man came back to me, not with doubts, but fully convinced that Jesus Christ never rose from the dead.

How strong is our belief? What kind of job are we doing in the church? Are we able to describe to others the Christian faith in understandable terms? Do we cease learning about God? Do we give up on people and say, "What's the use — she'll never believe"? It is time we Christians put our finger on the problem; we tend to give up on people and we are tempted to give up on God. Faith learning is a lifetime opportunity. The Bible is a book of faith, God-given faith, and how this faith has worked in the everyday lives of ordinary people.

Thus, it is far better to be sure, to want to be sure about faith in God. After fighting through doubts, you will be a more confident person. God never commands that we eliminate doubts. God gives a faith wherein we can put our trust. It is far worse to profess a fuzzy faith than to face doubts. Fight through doubting until you reach your certainty of God: "My Lord and my God!"

It is marvelous that Jesus chose a person like Thomas, another fisherman from the area of Galilee.

Matthew, Mark, and Luke tell us nothing about Thomas except his name. John's Gospel reveals the character of Thomas. The name *Thomas* is the Hebrew. He is also called *Didymus* which is the Greek for a twin. If he was a twin, we do not hear anything of his brother or sister.

Thomas was more than a doubter, however; he had determination. Recall the story of Lazarus. Jesus was told that Lazarus was ill. To go back to where Lazarus lived meant considerable risk, for twice in that area Jesus faced the danger of being stoned to death. (See John 8:59; 10:31.) The other disciples did not want to go to Bethany, a few miles from Jerusalem. The religious authorities had already determined that Jesus should die. It seemed the other disciples would not go. It was Thomas who said, "Let us also go, that we may die with him" (John 11:16).

A person of commitment, Thomas did not let danger determine a course of action. What was right to do was correct regardless of consequence. If Thomas was a pessimist, it would have been difficult for him to make such a statement. Instead, Thomas was rallying the other disciples to go up to Jerusalem. Without Thomas, Christ might have faced Jersualem alone. Without Thomas there might not have been the Lord's Supper, or a record of Gethsemane.

But the crucifixion did something to Thomas, a kind of burnout. He was not around when Jesus first appeared to the disciples after the resurrection. Like a wounded animal, he must have gone off alone and suffered.

But Thomas came back and was there when Jesus appeared to the disciples a second time. The testimony of his friends altered Thomas' view. When he made his confession, no doubts remained; faith reigned. It was to this band of believers a command was given, "As the Father has sent me, even so I send you" (John 20:21).

What happened to Thomas after that? The New Testament does not give us clues; tradition does.

One tradition asserts that Thomas proclaimed the good news in Parthia, an independent kingdom which stretched from the Indus to the Tigris, and from the Persian Gulf to the Caspian Sea. The Parthians were known as an independent people that even the Romans respected and feared.

Another tradition has Thomas preaching the gospel "... to the Parthians, Medes, Persians, Carmanians, Hyrcanians, Bactrians and Magians...."[1] Some say he went on to China. When he returned to India, he was stoned and finally killed with a sword. Vasco da Gama reported finding Christian relics there purported to be of Thomas. When I was in India, I found churches and crosses in honor of Thomas. It was to St. Thomas Church in Calcutta, that the late Sister Teresa's body was taken for viewing.

Now turn to Matthew. As we do, tell me who is number one on your hate list? The IRS?! Yourself? A lot of people do not like themselves. I always wondered what Matthew thought of himself. Before he became an apostle, he was a tax collector.

It would be hard to imagine a hate deeper and with more cause than the Jews' hatred for Roman tax collectors. Records indicate there were two kinds of tax collectors: first, there was the *Gabba*, who collected the statutory taxes such as ground tax — one tenth of your grain crop; one fifth of your wine, fruit, and oil; one percent of your income; a poll tax of one denarii per year, paid by all males between the ages of fourteen and 65 and by all females between the ages of twelve and 65.

The second was the *Mokhes*. This tax collector could stop anybody anywhere at any time and demand to see the goods being carried. He could search anybody, except married women. He could collect these taxes: import and export (two and one half to twelve and one half percent of the value); purchase tax on anything bought or sold; bridge tax whenever one crossed a bridge; road tax on main roads; harbor tax whenever one entered a harbor; town tax whenever a traveler entered a walled town; taxes on crossing rivers, on ships, on dams; license fees for certain trades; and so on.

These *Mokhes* had been known to stop a man on the road and force him to open his baggage and strip off his clothing, and then impose any kind of tax he liked. They were known to assess a duty impossible for a person to pay and then offer a loan at an impossible rate of interest!

No wonder the Roman government was despised, as were those who collected for them. To top it off, the strict Jew felt that to pay tribute money to anyone other than God was to infringe upon his/ her belief. Thus, a tax collector went against the grain of the Jew's religion, his conscience, and his self-respect. Tax collectors were hated, classified in the same breath with Gentiles, harlots, and informers.

In such an unpopular business was Matthew — a man whom everyone despised. How the Jews hated him!

Think of what it meant for Jesus to call a tax collector to become one of his followers! It did not seem to matter to Jesus. There Matthew sat at the tax office at Capernaum. Jesus said to him, "Follow me." And Matthew did. He even arranged dinner in his own home in Jesus' honor "... and there was a large crowd of tax collectors and others sitting at the table with them" (Luke 5:29). I doubt Matthew had many friends other than tax collectors and so-called "others." But Matthew's friends gladly listened to what Jesus had to say.

However, it seemed Matthew jumped from the frying pan into the fire. His more practical friends could have said to him, "Are you crazy? Giving up a tax collector's lucrative income to follow a dreamer like that!" His relatives could have complained, "If you were going to change jobs, you could have at least found something more profitable than religion!"

And can you not hear others saying: "Matthew? The tax collector? Who is he trying to fool with a cloak of religion? He's not in it for nothing! He's like those in government. He'll be paid handsomely by Rome for infiltrating."

If you have ever changed jobs, you know something of how Matthew felt. At one point in my life I felt called away from a parish and accepted a position with a university. My motives were questioned. Unkind judgments were made.

When Matthew rose and followed Christ, no doubt Matthew had observed Jesus carefully. He heard Jesus preach. He analyzed what following Jesus meant. And when the invitation came to be with Christ in his ministry, Matthew did not hesitate. "He got up, left everything, and followed him" (Luke 5:28).

Matthew could have remained a tax collector and become a Christian. We do not have to give up our work to follow Jesus Christ. He wants you and me to be Christian where we work — honest and upright and bringing others so that Christ's word can come to bear.

Matthew used his business experience in his discipleship. Other disciples were not good with the pen. Matthew was. Because of his writing we have the first Gospel.

What a contribution Matthew made! Unpopular most of his life, experiencing the white heat of hatred, he left the world richer by his pen. One cannot read the Book of Matthew without realizing that here was a person who understood Jesus' mission, a person who experienced a change in perspective and purpose in life. All hate of self must have gone out of Matthew as he recorded Jesus' words of eternal life.

After the resurrection, there is good reason to believe Matthew preached the gospel in Judea to his own people. Then tradition has him in Ethiopia, Persia, Parthia, Macedonia, and other places. There is a tradition that he was condemned by the Sanhedrin, and another that he was martyred in Egypt.

From the lives of Thomas and Matthew, we learn:

1) It is good to wade through doubts before embracing the faith.

2) It is meaningful to be in the company of believers when grief strikes.

3) Although the resurrection cannot be proven, it cannot be disproven, and only faith can embrace belief in life with God forever.

4) God chose ordinary people to follow him, even people with doubts or those caught in an unsavory occupation.

5) It takes trust in Jesus to follow him all the way into eternity.

6) We may have to switch occupations or direction along the way, if we are going to follow Christ.

7) Following Christ means surrendering every area of life to him.

8) Determination is a valued trait.

Questions For Discussion

1. Can you be a Christian and still harbor doubts?

2. What can be done about doubts?

3. What do you say to a person who has difficulty believing in the resurrection?

4. Has anybody ever gone away from the church and then returned? What happened?

5. What can be done about prejudice? How do we handle hatred?

6. In an era of job insecurity, what effect does insecurity have upon a person?

7. Can you be a Christian and popular at the same time? Are there times when we risk being popular?

---

1. According to Jerome's Lives, quoted by William Barclay, *The Master's Men* (Abingdon Press), p. 51.

Chapter 6

The Lives Of Simon, The Zealot; James, The Son Of Alphaeus; And Thaddaeus

The lives of the apostles tell us much about the mind of Jesus. Jesus did not select "yes" people as followers. Not only did the apostles differ in background and personality, they differed in their philosophy of life. We see this quite pointedly in the lives of these three apostles. If we understand the word *zealot,* we will better understand these three men.

Consider Simon, the Zealot. *Zealot,* in Hebrew, derived from the verb *Kana,* means "to be jealous" or eager for an enterprise. *Zealot* in Greek means to be "jealous of the law." From this brief word background we gain insight into the philosophy of life which Simon embraced before becoming a follower of Jesus. Since the scriptures tell us so little about him, except listing him as one of the twelve, it is necessary for us to understand just what a zealot stood for and what motivated Simon in his pre-apostolic days.

As we know history, Palestine was under the rule of Rome. *Time* magazine on one of its covers had the caption "Troubled Israel — Military Tensions, Chaotic Economy, Election Showdown." It is like that today. It was not unlike that in Jesus' day. There were tensions in the Holy Land.

Although there were a few years of comparative tranquility, especially under Herod the Great who combined charisma with the art of diplomacy, the Jews never did accept Roman rule. The Holy Land has always been like a volcano, subject to eruption.

The Zealots were fervent patriots. In a real sense, the Zealots could be termed fanatical. They eventually became terrorists. They were called the *Sicarii* — the assassins — the name derived from *sici,* a little curved sword which could be carried underneath their clothing and could be whipped out at a moment's notice. They hated Rome with a vengeance. And, if any Jew was thought to compromise with Rome, such a person, although a Jew, was marked for assassination. It resembles the McCarthy era in the United States a few decades ago when almost anyone was suspected of having some communistic connection. It also sounds like the terrorists of today.

The Masada story tells about the Zealots. I went up that mountain and gazed over the Dead Sea, and I was amazed how the Zealots must have lived atop that mountain. They were the last of the Zealots following the devastating siege of Jerusalem in A.D. 70. Eleazar, the commander of the Masada group, made sure the Romans did not enjoy their "victory " when it became clear the end was near. Much like Jim Jones at Guyana and the group in San Diego which committed mass suicide, Eleazar was able to convince the men of Masada to kill their own wives and children and then commit suicide. It is stated in *Wars Of The Jews* that "they tenderly embraced their wives, kissed their children, and then began the bloody work. Nine hundred and sixty perished; only two women and five children escaped by hiding in a cave."[1]

The Zealots at Masada in the first century have motivated modern Israel. Their national motto is "Never give up." They even take their new recruits atop the mountain and indoctrinate them with the philosophy of what happened at Masada. On that mountain these recruits take their vows of loyalty.

We cannot say that Simon the Zealot was all of these things. But this is the background of the man. He was devoted to the law, hated Rome, and was a nationalist of the most dangerous kind.

Why did Jesus select him? For whatever reason, it is amazing that Jesus could keep peace among the twelve. Matthew, a tax collector, represented a "fellow traveler" with Rome as far as Simon was concerned. I wonder what it was like when Matthew and Simon met for the first time. I wonder if Simon curled his fingers around his *sica* hidden underneath his robe. I wonder if he ever thought of killing Matthew for the "cause."

It demonstrates the powerful force of Christ's presence and his message of love. It makes us want to believe that Christ can bring any two opposing forces together and cause those involved to live in peace. Israel could use his presence now. This love that symbolizes the life of Christ can work among different personalities. We need to try this at our work and/or at home.

Acts 1:13 tells us that Simon the Zealot was with the other disciples after the Ascension of our Lord. His life had changed. He became a cross-bearer instead of a knife-bearer.

They say that Simon preached in Egypt, Africa, and possibly in Britain. Legend has him even in Persia, where he was supposedly attacked by fanatics of a different kind — religious fanatics — and was killed. Simon and Thaddaeus evidently made some missionary journeys together. They had held the same philosophy of life before they became apostles and therefore might have felt closer to one another.

Take a quick look at the life of Thaddaeus. Thaddaeus had as many as three names, not uncommon in those days. In Mark 3:18 he is called Thaddaeus. In Matthew 10:3 (King James Translation) he is called Lebbaeus whose surname was Thaddaeus; in Luke he is called Judas, the brother or son of James (Luke 6:16 and Acts 1:13). We can be confident that all three names refer to Thaddaeus.

Thaddaeus is known only for the one question he asked of Jesus recorded in John 14:22-23. He asks, " 'Lord, how is it that you will reveal yourself to us, and not to the world?' Jesus answered him, 'Those who love me will keep my word, and my Father will love them, and we will come to them and make our home with them.' "

Thaddaeus, like Simon, was a nationalist. He wanted Jesus to go public and prove to the world that he was God. This is a reflection of the Zealot stance. In effect, Jesus told Thaddaeus that that is not the way the world is won. You cannot make people believe; you can only give them the opportunity to believe. The surrendered life is the best life of all.

We have a tough time learning that God's way may be better than ours. It is not easy to turn one's life over to someone one cannot see. It is not easy to surrender. Surrender is another name for love.

There is a beautiful legend about Thaddaeus. He is supposed to have gone to Edessa, a city of northwest Mesopotamia, where he healed the disease of a king as well as many of the citizens. The king offered Thaddaeus silver and gold but Thaddeus refused the money. He is supposed to have said, "If we have forsaken that which is our own, how shall we take that which is another's?" This statement reflects the attitude of the apostles. They were not concerned for their own welfare but for the welfare of others. Any ordained person today worth his/her salt embraces that philosophy. And any Christian would be well advised to do the same.

Thaddaeus went on to preach in other places and is supposed to have gone to Ararat where he was killed with arrows.

We come to James, the son of Alphaeus, the least known of all the apostles. The Bible only lists his name in Matthew 10:3, Mark 3:18, Luke 6:15, and Acts 1:13.

One thing we do know about him is that he was the brother of Matthew. We know this because Mark records, "And as he (Jesus) passed on, he saw Levi the son of Alphaeus sitting at the tax office ... (Mark 2:14). Levi was also called Matthew. So Matthew and James had the same father, Alphaeus. James may have been the younger. Two different philosophies were represented in the same family. Like Simon, James could have been tempted to pull a knife on his brother, Matthew.

Here again we see the powerful influence of Christ on human life. Reconciliation comes into the family of Alphaeus. Brothers with decidedly different viewpoints, opposed to one another, are brought together under the same roof of reconciling love. It is likely that each gave witness to this fact in his preaching. Is not that the role of the Christian — to be a reconciler?

The last four disciples (including Judas Iscariot) are frequently lumped together. It is likely they all had something in common and that common factor could have been that they had been zealots before becoming apostles.

James preached in Syria and in Russia. He was martyred for his beliefs. Because we do not know much about this James, he is called the patron saint of the nameless.

We learn these lessons from the lives of these three apostles — Simon, James, and Thaddaeus:

1) We dare not equate or confuse patriotism with Christianity. Christ did not come to rule the world; he came to rule the world's heart.

2) There is a time to stand up for human rights. However, we can stand up not with the power of hate or force but with the power of love and gentle persuasion.

3 God selects all sorts and conditions of people to serve him. Everybody is eligible.

4) Surrendering your life to Christ is not abdication of happiness; it is an act of purposeful living which brings joy beyond the capacity of the so-called "pursuit of happiness." Happiness pursues a person with a right relationship with God and others.

5) It is okay to ask questions of God; it is also good to listen to his answers. This takes time and energy. It takes time to be still and know God. Such answers could result in the change of life's direction.

6) Never underestimate the power and influence of Christian love. It can bring child and parent, husband and wife, brother and sister together, even if different philosophies prevail. We all see life differently when we listen to each other, another dimension of God's gift.

7) Very likely you will not be called upon to sacrifice your life for the cause of Christ, as these apostles did. However, Christians in China and other parts of the world are being persecuted today. All of us are called to live lives reflecting the fact that we are part of God's family.

Questions For Discussion

1. These three disciples seemed to have played a lesser role among the twelve. Were they less important?

2. What contribution, if any, can a person make when considered less important than others?

3. What importance do we attach to support of certain political parties? If you are a Republican, do you look upon a Democrat with suspicion, or vice versa?

4. Is it right for missionaries to promote democracy in other countries? What is right for them to do?

5. Most of us are not well-known. Does this affect our Christian witness?

6. Is the force of Christian love stronger than the force of evil?

7. What happens to us when we harbor hatred?

8. What kind of role models are we? What kind should we be?

---

1. *Wars Of The Jews*, pp. 7-9.

Chapter 7

The Life Of Judas Iscariot

Are you a good judge of character? I always thought I was — that is, until I met Sam.

Sam appeared for worship one Sunday night at the new mission church I was serving in San Mateo, California, my first parish. Sam needed help. His mother had died and he had no money to get to the funeral in San Diego, 500 miles down the road.

At first, I thought Sam was a big liar. I should have kept to my first hunch! Anyway, after worship we piled Sam into our automobile, took him to our home, and put him up for the night. (Times have changed. It would be dangerous to do that today.) During the evening conversation in our home, which lasted into the night, Sam knew people I knew, as far away as the east. He documented incidents of a personal nature. And Sam could outpray anybody I had ever met. When he got down on his knees and let the words flow, I thought Jesus was coming back in person right then and there.

The next morning, after a hearty breakfast, I took Sam to the train station, bought him a ticket to San Diego, and saw him off to his mother's funeral. "There's my good deed for the day," I thought to myself. But just to make sure it was a good deed, I put a tracer on the ticket. In due time I learned Sam had gotten off at the next station and cashed in the ticket. Since that time I have questioned my ability to judge character!

Of couse, I should not lose all faith in humanity because one person betrayed me. Jesus did not give up on people because Judas turned out to be a traitor. Jesus did not turn his head away from the thief on the cross who asked to be remembered. He answered that man's prayer by giving him assurance of eternal life. We should be thankful that God does not give up on us because of our sins.

I can understand Sam now. He was a professional huckster. He betrayed my confidence. Judas Iscariot was not like that. What was Judas Iscariot really like?

Scholars weave together one story after another about the meaning of his name. One says his name means he came from Jericho. Another says his name means "reward." Still another connects his name with leather and that he had a leather coat with pockets which could easily hold the thirty pieces of silver given to him by the authorities for betraying Jesus.

The most likely meaning of his name is that he was from Kerioth. Kerioth is in southern Judea. If this is so, Judas Iscariot was the only disciple *not* from Galilee. Did this make him feel like an outsider? Who could feel like that in the presence of Christ? Nevertheless, it is a thought worth considering.

What is far more worth considering is that Judas Iscariot was a good disciple. He had a thrifty sense about him. When Mary of Bethany anointed Jesus' feet with a costly ointment, he protested: "Why was this perfume not sold for three hundred denarii and the money given to the poor?" (John 12:5). An addendum in the Bible indicates this amount would be worth a laborer's annual pay. In today's market, that would be like wasting several dozens of bottles of Chanel No. 5 perfume. Judas was a good treasurer, despite John's comment that he was a thief (which John wrote in later years as he looked back upon the life of Judas). Whether Judas did put his hand in the till nobody knows. If he did, what could he have used the money for? And why would the others continue to trust him with their money since Jesus and the disciples had everything in common? The fact is that Judas had a monetary sense of value. Jesus judged this quality correctly and made him treasurer.

Furthermore, Judas had a deep feeling for people. He did not like to see his people treated like Roman puppets. He could have sung our song of America with gusto: "... let freedom ring."

As a consequence, there is every good reason to believe that Judas wanted Jesus to be king. After the five thousand were fed and the people wanted to make Jesus king, Judas would have been the one to put a crown on his head. When Jesus rode triumphantly into Jerusalem, and the roadway was paved with palm branches,

Judas' hosanna could have been heard above the others. He believed in Jesus. He believed Jesus had the qualities to rule the world. If James and John wanted to be on his left and right, that was okay, but Judas was more concerned that Jesus become king of all.

Judas had the potential of being the apostle Jesus meant him to be: a treasurer, who enjoyed the trust of Christ and the disciples; a man of vision, who wanted the highest place for his Lord. Jesus chose a good man in Judas. It was an excellent choice of character. But what went wrong? What made Judas betray Jesus? The human mind is certainly complicated, isn't it? Who can understand Aaron Burr or Benedict Arnold or Vidkun Quisling of Norway in World War II, or one of our best secret service men giving away top secrets to the Kremlin?

We cannot rightly analyze the motives of Judas. Before we even begin to examine them we must say to ourselves, "Let anyone among you who is without sin be the first to throw a stone ..." (John 8:7).

Outwardly, Judas must have been the same as the other disciples. We cannot say exactly what made him turn on Jesus. If he conceived of Jesus as a political emancipator, he could have been bitterly disappointed that Jesus did not accept the crown when offered. If he harbored political ambition for himself, his love for Christ could have turned into hate.

Mark Rutherford (pseudomym of William Hale White, English novelist, 1829-1913) wrote: "Can any position be more irritating than that of a careful man of business who is keeper of the purse for a company of heedless enthusiasts professing complete indifference to the value of money, misunderstanding the genius of their chief, and look out every morning for some sign in the clouds, a prophecy of their immediate appointment as viceregents of a power that would supersede the awful majesty of the imperial city?"[1]

Judas' main trouble was this: he tried to fit Christ into his own plan. He would have used the expensive perfume another way. He would have Christ exercise his Lordship by asserting divine power. Judas would set Jesus up by having him arrested so that Jesus would be forced finally to declare his messiahship.

49

Whatever motive or motives Judas had, he was wrong. We cannot make God over into what we want him to be. Jesus refused to be what Judas wanted him to be. An echo from Isaiah 55:8 rings in our ears, "For my thoughts are not your thoughts, nor are your ways my ways, says the Lord." That is hard to learn, let alone remember.

Jesus gave Judas every opportunity to change his mind. At the last supper the disciples had with Jesus, Judas is given his usual place among the twelve. In fact, Judas, although not one of the three closest associates of Jesus (as Peter, James, and John), was well thought of among the twelve and Jesus. We know this by the arrangement of persons at the supper.

In those days dinner guests reclined on couches. They would lean on their left elbows and eat with their right hands. (I do not know what they did if they were lefthanded!) Couches held three persons. The most favored person was to the left of the host. In this way the host's head would be near the chest of the person on the left. Judas was on the left. Jesus said to the disciples that "... one of you will betray me." Judas had the temerity to ask, "Surely not I, Lord?" (Matthew 26:21, 22).

There were three items on the table at the passover feast. First, there was a paste called *charosheth* made of apples, dates, pomegranates, and nuts. This symbolized the clay used in making bricks which the Israelites had to make as slaves of Egypt. This paste reminded them of their days of slavery. Then there were bitter herbs — endive, horseradish, chicory, and horehound — which reminded them of the bitterness of slavery. The unleavened bread was a reminder of how quickly they had to get out of Egypt. They did not have time to bake leavened bread but carried dough and kneading troughs with them so that they could bake as they traveled. I have seen Bedouins do this today.

During the passover ceremony, they put the herbs between two pieces of unleavened bread, dipped it into the *charosheth*, and ate. This was called sop. For a host to prepare the sop and give it to a guest was a sign of honor. Jesus did this for Judas (John 13:26). It is very possible that because Jesus and Judas were in such close proximity, Jesus could have said in private to Judas the words, "Do quickly what you are going to do" (John 13:27). If the other disciples really knew that Judas was going to betray Jesus, it is doubtful Judas would have gotten out of the room!

It is too bad about Judas — name defamed and never reaching his potential. After the betrayal, the man realized what he had done but it was too late. He tried to give the money back but the priests would not have anything to do with tainted money. Tainted money or blood money was only good to buy a potter's field — a place to bury strangers. (See Matthew 27:6-10.)

A. B. Bruce seems to sum up Judas' life: "He was bad enough to do the deed of infamy, and good enough to be unable to bear the burden of his guilt."[2] Yes, Judas hanged himself.

It is all in our perspective. Do we seek an out in life by suicide or do we face life even if it has a cross? The greatest tragedy on Good Friday was not the crucifixion of Jesus Christ — that was tragically necessary. The greatest tragedy was Judas' taking things into his own hands again, trying to make things turn out his own way. This was the real betrayal — that Christ was not given the opportunity to forgive and redeem Judas.

The new Church to be born on Pentecost could have used a good treasurer; the new Church could have used a person of vision. Our Lord could have made a real disciple of him, a person willing to give his life instead of taking it. Tragically, Judas never reached his potential.

We learn these things from the life of Judas:

1)   Keep respect for humankind even if some people deceive you.

2)   Ask God to mold your life instead of doing it on your own.

3)   Accept forgiveness for failures and misunderstandings — forgiveness from the Savior who poured out his blood for you so that you could be forgiven.

4)   Let God be God. Refrain from trying to force issues which should be left in the hands of God.

5)   When Jesus looks at you as he must have looked at Judas, don't try to cover up with a question, "Is it I, Lord?" You and I know very well when we betray Jesus.

6)   Strive to live up to your potential.

There is no escape in a hangman's tree. There is certain hope through Calvary's tree.

Questions For Discussion

1.   Was Frank Sinatra's song title "I Did It My Way," correct?

2.   When do we try to force God's hand in doing it "my way"?

3.   Is prayer an attempt to make God come around to our way of thinking?

4.   Is suicide a forgivable sin?

5.   What is our potential?

---

1. Cited by William Barclay, *The Master's Men* (Abingdon Press), p. 77.

2. A. B. Bruce, *The Training Of The Twelve*, p. 367 and in *The Dictionary Of Christ And The Gospels, Volume I*, p. 912.

Chapter 8

The Life Of Paul

Paul was not one of the twelve. He never met Jesus in person but is called an apostle because of his missionary efforts. Paul experienced faith as we expectantly hope to do on some Damascus road.

Paul was a person of three worlds: the world of the Jew, the world of the Gentile, the world of Christianity. We understand something of this apostle if we understand these three worlds.

Unmistakably, Paul was a Jew, Through the centuries there has not been much love for the Jew. In the day of Paul, this was doubly true. Cicero called the Jewish religion "a barberous superstitution."[1] Tacitus called the Jewish nation "the vilest of people."[2] As William Barclay described it, "The world hated them and they hated the world."[3]

Thus, anti-semitism is nothing new. It was rampant in Paul's time, as in ours. Then imagine Christianity stemming out of Judaism! How difficult it must have been for a Jew to take this "new" religion to all the world. It would have been difficult for a Gentile, let alone a Jew, to do this. It would also have been difficult to convince the Jew, who believed he was of the chosen people, that Jesus was really and truly the Messiah. Such a person was Paul. After his own conversion, he was able to contribute to the conversion of both Gentile and Jew. Without Paul, Christianity might never have captivated the world. That is how important one life can be!

Paul never apologized for being a Jew. He makes claim for it in 2 Corinthians 11:22: "Are they Hebrews? So am I. Are they Israelites? So am I. Are they descendants of Abraham? So am I."

When Paul states he is a Hebrew, he is saying he still speaks the language. The Jews of the Dispersion had forgotten their language. When he says he is an Israelite, he means he is a part of the nation that has a covenant with God. When he announces he is of the seed of Abraham, he is tracing his personal history back to the tribe of Benjamin. Nobody is purer Jew that he is, Paul claims.

All through Paul's writings, he keeps making reference to his Jewish heritage. He says in his defense at Jerusalem after an arrest, "I am a Jew, born at Tarsus in Cilicia, but brought up in this city at the feet of Gamaliel, educated strictly according to our ancestral law ..." (Acts 22:3).

So, Paul was able to communicate within the Jewish world. He did not abandon Judaism; he built upon it and made Christ the cornerstone.

But Paul was not a one-world person. He could communicate not only in the Jewish world but in the Gentile world. In his defense before King Agrippa at Caesarea, he made claim to have been sent to preach to the Gentiles. Even King Agrippa exclaimed, "Are you so quickly persuading me to become a Christian?" (Acts 26:28). Paul makes the same claim to the Galatians (Galatians 1:16). In Ephesians he speaks of himself as a prisoner of the Lord for the Gentiles (Ephesians 3:1, 8). In 1 and 2 Timothy he is a teacher of the Gentiles. Paul was able to communicate within the Gentile world.

The Book of Acts is our source of his life. His letters, unlike the "me" books of today, do not record his life story. Others must tell it for him.

He was born in Tarsus. Tarsus dated as far back as 860 B. C. Shalmaneser of Assyria named it as one of his conquests. Alexander the Great bathed in the icy water of its river (Cydnus) and almost died from a chill. Mark Anthony stayed in Tarsus preparing for war against the Parthians. Cleopatra made her famous boat trip to Tarsus to visit Mark Anthony. So Paul was a citizen of "an important city" (Acts 21:39). There he learned how to make tents. There he received his Roman citizenship. There he acquired his cosmopolitan touch. Paul was a unique person; he could speak to both Jew and Gentile.

It is in the Christian world that we know him best of all. He was present at the stoning of Stephen. He was a persecutor of the Jerusalem church before he became a Christian. On a persecuting trip to Damascus he was converted to the Christian faith. He used his knowledge of the law and his faith given by Christ in making three missionary journeys that established churches that were to change the world. He experienced shipwrecks, beatings, and imprisonment. He was arrested in Jerusalem, appealed to Caesar as the right of a Roman citizen, and was shipped to Rome for trial. Strangely enough the author of Acts does not tell us of the death of Paul. As a Roman citizen, however, he would not have been crucified — he would have been beheaded. Origen wrote that Paul was martyred under Nero. Eusebius, the historian of later years (326), believed this also was the end of Paul's life.

If anyone would describe the life of Paul he would have to include these words: clear thinker, conversion experience, evangelism thrust, truth always, inward peace, tenderhearted, fighter, physically unattractive, conflict, anxiety, city life, the arena, the court, the military, spontaneity, sarcasm, irony, denunciation, exuberance, gospel, the church.

Stalker's *Life Of St. Paul* puts his life in perspective:

> *He lives among us today with a life a hundredfold more influential than that which throbbed in his brain whilst the earthly form which made him visible still lingered on the earth. Wherever the feet of them who publish the glad tidings go forth beautiful upon the mountains, he walks by their side as an inspirer and a guide; in ten thousand churches every sabbath and on a thousand thousand hearths every day his eloquent lips still teach that gospel of which he was never ashamed; and, wherever there are human souls searching for the white flower of holiness or climbing the difficult heights of self-denial, there he whose life was so pure, whose devotion to Christ was so entire, and whose pursuit of a single purpose was so unceasing, is welcome as the best of friends.*[4]

Gunther Bornkamm in his book titled *Paul* very likely sums up the life of Paul with a quote from Paul himself from 2 Corinthians 4:7, "But we have this treasure in earthen vessels...." In Paul we have both an earthen vessel and a treasure. He developed Christian thought. His treasure is our theology. The disciples did not have that capacity. Paul, the educated, articulate person, has given the world the good news in black and white. Luther was brought to his knees by Paul's writings (Romans), and in turn brought the Church back to its knees. And today, when an individual or church gets off track, the writings of Paul can bring people back to spiritual sanity.

We learn these things from the life of Paul:

1) One person can make a difference. A situation or a world stance can be redirected by one life committed to the Lord Jesus Christ.

2) Life may turn out to be a turn around. When we are headed in one direction, God may have a different idea. Listen to God whether it be the stroke of the sun or a seared conscience.

3) Speak up for Christ wherever you are despite the consequence.

4) Endure suffering with faith.

5) Do not capitulate to falsehood.

8) Be faithful unto death.

Questions For Discussion

1. Review Stephen's testimony and death and the persecution of the church in Acts 6-8. What impact was made upon Paul at the stoning of Stephen?

2. What was Saul like? What education did he have? A Ph.D.? Why was he so intent about the law of Moses? Why was his name changed to Paul?

3. Describe Paul's conversion in Acts 9:1-19; 22:6-21; 26:12-18. Has anybody here been converted?

4. What was Paul's thorn in the flesh as described in 2 Corinthians 12:7?

5. Why were the missionary journeys of Paul so important?

6. Why do we look to Paul for our theology?

---

1. *Cicero, Pro Flasso 28*, cited by William Barclay, *The Mind Of Paul*, p. 9.

2. *Tacitus, Histories 5:8, Ibid.*

3. *Ibid.*

4. James Stalker, *Life Of St. Paul* (Fleming H. Revell Co., 1912), pp. 143-144.